Simple Wonders

PAINTINGS BY

*Kathryn
Andrews
Fincher*

HARVEST HOUSE PUBLISHERS
EUGENE, OREGON 97402

Simple Wonders

Copyright © 1998 Harvest House Publishers
Eugene, Oregon 97402

ISBN 1-56507-810-1

All works of art reproduced in this book are copyrighted by Kathryn Andrews Fincher and are reproduced under license from © Arts Uniq®, Inc., Cookeville, TN. For information regarding art prints featured in this book, please contact:

Arts Uniq'
P.O. Box 3085
Cookeville TN 38502
800-223-5020

Design and production by Garborg Design Works, Minneapolis, Minnesota

Harvest House Publishers has made every effort to trace the ownership of all poems and quotes. In the event question arising from the use of any poem or quote, we regret any error made and will be pleased to make the cessary correction in future editions of this book.

Manufactured in China.

98 99 00 01 02 03 04 05 06 07 / IM / 10 9 8 7 6 5 4 3 2 1

To look at the world through the eyes of a child is to see delight in small things, amazement in ordinary things, and wonder in all things. Enjoy this age of innocence again. Enjoy these simple wonders.

Wonder is especially proper to childhood, and it is the sense of wonder above all that keeps us young.

GERALD VANN

One summer I had my pony at Fern Quarry....I spent many of my happiest hours on his back. Occasionally, when it was quite safe, my teacher would let go the leading-rein, and the pony sauntered on or stopped at his sweet will to eat grass or nibble the leaves of the trees that grew beside the narrow trail...ah me! How well I remember the spicy, clovery smell of his breath!

HELEN KELLER

The fruit of the Spirit is joy.
THE BOOK OF GALATIANS

It has long been an

axiom of mine that the

little things are infinitely

the most important.

SIR ARTHUR CONAN DOYLE

8

And now my memory fondly plays

Around the haunts of boyhood days—

The days made up of fairy dreaming—

The days with joy and hope full teeming.

When nature seemed more fair by far,

In light of sun and twinkling star;

When every flower and shrub and tree

Seemed made for happiness—and me!

JULIAN SHALLCROSS

Isn't it splendid to think of all the things there are to find out about? It just makes me feel glad to be alive—it's such an interesting world. It wouldn't be half so interesting if we knew all about everything, would it? There'd be no scope for imagination, would there?

L.M. MONTGOMERY

Anne of Green Gables

Stop and consider God's wonders.

THE BOOK OF JOB

Teacher says you want to know what kind of pet I would
like to have. I love all living things; I suppose everybody
does. But of course, I cannot have a menagerie. I have a
big, beautiful pony and a large dog. And I would like a
little dog to hold in my lap, or a big pussy (there are no fine
cats in Tuscumbia), or a parrot. I would like to feel a parrot
talk. It would be so much fun. But I would be pleased with
and love any little creature you send me.

HELEN KELLER
From a Letter to a Friend

A happy face makes

a glad heart.

THE BOOK OF PROVERBS

So wherever I am, there's always Pooh,
There's always Pooh and Me.
"What would I do?" I said to Pooh,
"If it wasn't for you," and Pooh said: "True,
It isn't much fun for One, but Two
Can stick together," says Pooh, says he.
"That's how it is," says Pooh.

A.A. MILNE

14

To get the full value of a joy you must have somebody to divide it with.

MARK TWAIN

15

Fix your thoughts on what is true and good and right. Think about things that are pure and lovely, and dwell on the fine, good things in others. Think about all you can praise God for and be glad about.

THE BOOK OF PHILIPPIANS

Being still too young to go often to the theater, and not rich enough to afford any great outlay for private performances, the girls put their wits to work and—necessity being the mother of invention—made whatever they needed. Very clever were some of their productions—pasteboard guitars, antique lamps made of old-fashioned butter boats covered with silver paper, gorgeous robes of old cotton, glittering with tin spangles from a pickle factory, and armor covered with the same useful diamond-shaped bits left in sheets when the lids of tin preserve pots were cut out. The furniture was used to being turned topsy-turvy, and the big chamber was the scene of many innocent revels.

LOUISA MAY ALCOTT

Little Women

Know you what it is

to be a child? It is

to...believe in love, to

believe in loveliness, to

believe in belief.

PERCY BYSSHE SHELLEY

20

Rain can't hurt us
No, indeed! Though fast it pour
From leaden skies above,
The big umbrella, as you see,
Quite large enough for two will be,
And dearly do they love—
These two—to hear the raindrops fall,
And patter overhead:
"For not a drop can fall on us!"
Laughs gleeful little Fred.
And Mamie cuddles close beside
Her manly little brother,
And says, "I ain't afraid, you see,
'Cause I've got Fred, and Fred's got me…"

AUTHOR UNKNOWN

How good is man's life, the mere

living! how fit to employ

All the heart and the soul and the

senses forever in joy.

ROBERT BROWNING

It is astonishing how short

a time it takes for very

wonderful things to happen.

FRANCES BURNETT

Backward, turn backward,

O Time, in your flight,

Make me a child again just

for tonight!

ELIZABETH AKERS ALLEN

"What a splendid day!" said Anne, drawing a long breath. "Isn't it good just to be alive on a day like this? I pity the people who aren't born yet for missing it. They may have good days, of course, but they can never have this one."

L.M. MONTGOMERY
Anne of Green Gables

Blessed are the simple,

for they shall have

much peace.

THOMAS À KEMPIS